POETRY ESCAPE

Break the silence, tell your truth.

WEST MIDLAND POETS

Edited By Elle Berry

To Lynda

Love Kian

xxx

First published in Great Britain in 2019 by:

YoungWriters

Young Writers
Remus House
Coltsfoot Drive
Peterborough
PE2 9BF
Telephone: 01733 890066
Website: www.youngwriters.co.uk

All Rights Reserved
Book Design by Spencer Hart
© Copyright Contributors 2019
SB ISBN 978-1-78988-546-0
Printed and bound in the UK by BookPrintingUK
Website: www.bookprintinguk.com
YB0405FZ

FOREWORD

Since 1991 our aim here at Young Writers has been to encourage creativity in children and young adults and to inspire a love of the written word. Each competition is tailored to the relevant age group, hopefully giving each student the inspiration and incentive to create their own piece of creative writing, whether it's a poem or a short story. We truly believe that seeing their work in print gives students a sense of achievement and pride.

For our latest competition *Poetry Escape*, we challenged secondary school students to free their creativity and break through the barriers to express their true thoughts, using poetic techniques as their tools of escape. They had several options to choose from offering either a specific theme or a writing constraint. Alternatively they could forge their own path, because there's no such thing as a dead end where imagination is concerned.

The result is an inspiring anthology full of ideas, hopes, fears and imagination, proving that creativity really does offer escape, in whatever form you need it.

We encourage young writers to express themselves and address topics that matter to them, which sometimes means exploring sensitive or difficult topics. If you have been affected by any issues raised in this book, details on where to find help can be found at: **www.youngwriters.co.uk/support**.

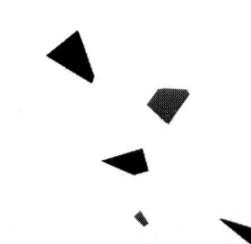

CONTENTS

Bishop Vesey's Grammar School, Sutton Coldfield

Krish Chauhan (11)	1
Charlotte Anna Robinson (17)	2
Timurs V (11)	4
Jamie Coley (12)	6
Ihram Tarafdar (12)	8
Owen Leigh (12)	9
Joseph Gorst (11)	10
Ethan Alexander Miller (11)	11
Harry Moors (11)	12
Ayaan Uppal (12)	13
Ollie James Barnes (11)	14
Sarvesh Mridul Leoprabhu (11)	15
Toby Critchley (11)	16
Matthew Arnold (12)	17
Oliver Ho (11)	18

Bishop Walsh Catholic School, Sutton Coldfield

Amy Mumford (11)	19

Ounsdale High School, Wombourne

Molly Hughes (13)	20
William Tyne (12)	23
Kieran Lavender (12)	24
Josh Stevens (12)	26
Grace Hollington (12)	28
Thomas Sidaway (13)	30
Kayleigh Barnett-West (14)	31
Lily May Morgan (12)	32
Harriet Ann Humpherson (11)	34
Lauren Paige Hodgkins (12)	36
Mark Cox (14)	38
Terrell Bennett (14)	40
Joe Conway-Lees (12)	42
James Price (12)	43
Niamh Carrothers (13)	44
Amelia Rowsell (12)	46
Kaiden Sidaway (12)	47
Suzie Aston (13)	48
Caitlyn Douch (14)	49
Evie Hollington (11)	50
Jack Lloyd (11)	51
Halle Glover (12)	52
Emily Roberts (12)	53
Noah Bradburn (13)	54
Mia White (14)	55
Eva Bradburn (12)	56
Charlotte Phillips (15)	57
Lillie Ann Perry (13)	58
Joshua Riley Thompson (12)	59
Ethan Lamsdale (11)	60
Megan Tune (12)	61
Nikita Crooke (12)	62
Layla Causer (12)	63
Joshua Edward Sanderson (11)	64
Emelia Grace Edwards (12)	65
Eve Lewis (13)	66
Emily Crump (15)	67
Jennie Louisa Stevens (12)	68
Willow Brittle (14)	69
Lily Collins (11)	70
Tom Priest (12)	71
Sophia Grinsell (12)	72
Kyla Williams (12)	73
Daniel Lowe (12)	74

Molly Rebecca Rabone (12)	75
Lottie May Beardsmore (11)	76
Alfie Thistle (12)	77
Daniel Jevons (12)	78
Michaela Tiniozou (12)	79
Keira Davies (12)	80
Tyrahan Singh Sandhu (12)	81
Harley Brook Trow (14)	82
Louise Walton (12)	83
Eden Randhawa (12)	84
Millie Georgina Smart (11)	85
Millie Grace Taylor (12)	86
Bethany Walker (12)	87

Our Lady & St Chad Catholic Academy, Wolverhampton

Julia Piechaczek (12)	88
Chloe Sereneo (11)	89
Caitlin Jefferis (11)	91

St Francis Of Assisi Catholic Technology College, Aldridge

Blaise Mich'eal River Delahunty-Forrest (12)	93
Marco Sadler (13)	94
James Culshaw (12)	97
Luca Sadler (12)	98
Violet-May Green (12)	101
Benita Jaeneke (12)	102
Erin McIntyre (13)	104
Sophie Doocey (13)	106
Amy Rose Weir (12)	108
Matthew Dowd (12)	110
Isabella Faye Rounds (13)	112
Alfie Stanley-Gough (12)	114
Arronveer Patter (12)	116
Phoebe Hastings (12)	118
Alex Richards (13)	120
Annie Hattersley (13)	122
Esther Omokorede (13)	124
Molly Abigail Cope (12)	126
Caitlin Hall (12)	127

Isabelle Welch (12)	128
Millie Anne Kilgallen (13)	129
Eilish O'Reilly	130
Dara Anderson (11)	131
Isobel Grant (11)	132
Naomi Aliu (12)	134
Millie Lavin	135
Sarah Morgan	136
Ethan Sivier (11)	137
Emilia Tilly Wassell (12)	138
Alisha Karvnanycike (13)	139
Kian Doody (11)	140
Aine-May Mulcrow (11)	141
Vivienne Ince (13)	142
Louie James Timmins (11)	143
Damian Biernacki (11)	144
Harrison Stage Murray (12)	145
Madeleine Relihan (12)	146
Sarone Mengisteab (11)	147
Cian James Hennessy (13)	148
Tamzin Timperley (12)	149
Henry Howell (11)	150
Emma Byrne (11)	151
Míceál Duggan-Wadehra (12)	152
Gabby Nolan (11)	153
Amelia Williams (12)	154
Holly Christine Mountford (12)	155
Sean Andrew Florence (12)	156
Harvey Williams-Castle (12)	157
Shantel Odera Dike (12)	158
Matthew John Logan (12)	159
Ryan Richards (13)	160
Erin Feely (12)	161
Charlotte Freeth (12)	162
Abigail Brookes (11)	163
Louise Kent (12)	164
Ashton Jones (11)	165
Aleksandra Chelchowska (12)	166
Erin Brown (11)	167
Freya Coyne (12)	168
Kelsey Leigh Harrison (12)	169
Eireann Mae Brannigan (12)	170
Callum O'Brien (12)	171

Serena Nunda (12) 172

The Coleshill School, Coleshill

Angus Glover (14) 173
Emily Taylor (13) 174

The Sixth Form College, Solihull

Melissa Allen (17) 176
Sophie Barnett (16) 178
Muhammad Ghulam Jamil (17) 180
Maia Winter (17) 182

THE POEMS

Pollution Must Stop

In time, pollution will end our world, we can't have this, we
can't have this
Many innocent animals die from this because we humans
can't simply put our plastic waste in the bin, we can't have
this, we can't have this
Our wildlife, Mother Nature has created with joy and
happiness, now getting destroyed with darkness and envy,
we can't have this, we can't have this
When every tree falls, there is pain and we can't have this,
we can't have this
When fossil fuels run free like a runaway kid, unfortunately,
our beloved world turns into a world without hope, we have
to stop this, we have to stop this
Our bulldozers and axes that are destroying our natural
beauties, is this supposedly making life better?
No!
We have to stop, help and protect our world, we only get
one after all.

Krish Chauhan (11)
Bishop Vesey's Grammar School, Sutton Coldfield

On Reminiscing

I remember the days that you would visit
Before the snow, sun and rain
I didn't realise how much I could miss it
Not that everything is not the same.
From the scintillating summer breeze that rippled through your clothes
To the transparent drops of cold that fell upon your face
Why has it changed? Where does love go?
I knew this would end, but I didn't know it was a race.
These lonely nights are treacherous
Far worse than any war I have known.
I am fading, it happens to the best of us
You'll realise this too when you've grown.
I've remained on this dishevelled rocking chair
Ever since you left, never to return
Staring out of the window in despair
I understand you've gone, but still, I yearn:
I yearn for company
I yearn for make-believe
But the more I yearn
The more I begin to seethe.
I hate these quiet days, evenings and nights
My imagination roams but I do not
When I first became ill, you told me to fight
And I did, but I'm still in this chair where you left me to rot!
I ought to have seen this from the start

The visits were occurring less and less
I'm in physical pain but the real pain is within my heart
I am simply one big mess.
But now, a decision I have to think about,
It's hard to love when love runs out
God, I wish we could go back to when we were younger.

Making paper planes, stargazing and games
Laughing at jokes that weren't even funny
Now nothing is the same
Even the sunny days aren't so sunny.

This is the last time my chair shall rock
Until it strikes twelve o'clock
I wish I could savour you before I am gone
But the clock's already striking: three, two, one...

Charlotte Anna Robinson (17)
Bishop Vesey's Grammar School, Sutton Coldfield

Global Warming

It is caused by us
And the local bus
And any other vehicles
Maybe even a bicycle

All those cows and pigs and chickens
And the horses and the llamas and the people
That produces all that waste
All of which creates unpleasant air taste
Pollutes the air even more

Cars, buses, trains, you name it!
All produce carbon dioxide
Which is bad for you
And mostly for the world too

This causes global warming
This causes icebergs melting
This causes countries flooding
This causes homelessness and migration
This causes more illnesses
This causes more unpleasant air
Which causes global warming!

It's an infinite loop
That we can break
If we try our best
The world we can make

With everything good
And *no* global warming
Nor disasters and
We can all be happy!

Timurs V (11)
Bishop Vesey's Grammar School, Sutton Coldfield

Misunderstanding

They think they know.
They don't.
They create rumours about us,
Disease. An incurable mental condition

They say we are idiots
They don't appreciate
That they are idiots too
They, like many, are wrong

Labels. Polluting the minds of
loads of children who are bullied
because of toxic
labels.

One in five, they say
have the disease. Disease
is known by its connotations.
Disease. They cower from us.

We are put down. Avoided. We
are talked about behind our backs
"So and so has this","so and so has that"
We cry. We hide. We cower

But we are reassured, we have a
superpower. We should
unite. Show the power. We are not
a disease. We are united...

Jamie Coley (12)
Bishop Vesey's Grammar School, Sutton Coldfield

World Peace

The word 'peace'
Like a dream that never came true
The words 'hunger, terrorism, bombing, fighting'
Words you instantly are familiarised with
Some say it's life, some don't care
But why should these be a part of our lives?
Why can't the news praise positives in this life?
Why do people sit at home feeling sorry for others when they could do much more?

Imagine if you could wake up every morning
Not a single dark cloud in your head
Not thinking about hundreds of people dying every day
A world with equality and without fighting
Where everyone has running water and food

Sometimes, dreams come true
I hope one day, this one does.

Ihram Tarafdar (12)
Bishop Vesey's Grammar School, Sutton Coldfield

Washed Away

The fish begin to cry
As creatures aplenty die
Their habitats destroyed
Away goes the life
Bit by bit, the problem grows
A hidden world mysterious with beauty
Wrecked into a wasteland
The garbage grows more

A shimmering blue universe
With infinite beauty
The wildlife grows
It flows across acres of sand
All of it we are yet to understand
But the mystery starts to die
The garbage grows more

A polluted land
It's no longer safe
Plastic dumped without a care
But soon, the water will fade away
It is poisonous to all life
Yet still, we cause the problem
The garbage grows more
As it's dumped in the ocean.

Owen Leigh (12)
Bishop Vesey's Grammar School, Sutton Coldfield

What I Hate ...

I hate inequality
And it has no integrity
I hate seeing people treated unfairly
This shouldn't happen, not even rarely

I hate bullying
I wish that people would let others do their own thing
I want to hit bullies, like a strike of lightning
And it's a problem that really needs fighting

I hate global warming
It's a problem that has been forming
Don't ruin the future for us
If you stop pollution, then we'll stop making a fuss

So please save society
Because this is the future for me
I'm filled with anxiety
When I see what horrors this wonderful world could be.

Joseph Gorst (11)
Bishop Vesey's Grammar School, Sutton Coldfield

Your Imagination

Your imagination is more special than you think
It can send you wherever you wanna go
It can create whoever you want to be
You must protect this important, powerful thing
And use it for the happy, adventurous thoughts

This is a place where the negatives are unheard
A place where you go if you're lonely or lost
Another life, but only better
Something that we can't make, we can't achieve
However, everyone owns a key to this extraordinary place
And opens the door to this imaginative space
Your imagination is more special than you think
Savour it as it's a special gift.

Ethan Alexander Miller (11)
Bishop Vesey's Grammar School, Sutton Coldfield

Just The Same

That man who sits down on the cobbled street,
He sits there, cold, with no shoes on his feet,
Is he not the same as I?

That black lady who's kicked and punched all night,
Surely she has exactly the same rights?
She must be the same as I.

That man who has wrinkles all on his face,
Every day he's in a frightening chase,
Could he be the same as I?

How you are born, you cannot change at all,
Make the most of your life, don't waste it all,
You are just the same as I.

Harry Moors (11)
Bishop Vesey's Grammar School, Sutton Coldfield

Tech

Tech is the new use,
In the modern days.
Used in public parties,
Used in many ways.

Playing games,
Writing notes,
Telling you which way to go.

Different software,
Different styles,
Different shops,
Going miles and miles.

Many uses in each place,
Driving
Playing
To the race!
Calling
Shooting your photos,
Oh! Here comes Santa
Ho ho ho!

The world goes crazy
Buying new tech,
Surfing
Searching
Watching Shrek.

Ayaan Uppal (12)
Bishop Vesey's Grammar School, Sutton Coldfield

War

War is a horrible thing
Only sadness does it bring
But down in the trenches are people with hearts of gold
Is it really fair that they're left fighting in the cold?

War is a place you could lose a brother
War is a place you could lose your mother
War is a place you could lose a friend
Don't worry, war is not the end

Because if we strive to work together
All these wars will stop forever
When war does finally cease
We can all live in timeless peace.

Ollie James Barnes (11)
Bishop Vesey's Grammar School, Sutton Coldfield

The Nature Is Dying

The lovely nature is dying
Trees are pleading and crying
The thick smoke is growing
The end of the world is approaching
This is what I am watching
The red, ferocious fire is roaring
There are no more children playing
The chainsaws have started piercing
Animals have started parting
Making new homes, they are starting
I can't believe what I am seeing
This really is happening
What I am seeing is not appealing
Global warming has started rising.

Sarvesh Mridul Leoprabhu (11)
Bishop Vesey's Grammar School, Sutton Coldfield

Stop Global Warning

Global warming is a warning
To us humans for emitting amounts of gas so appalling.
We are the main players
In breaking the ozone layer.

If we stop using harmful sources of power
We'll avoid the acid showers
Caused by air pollution
That are going to lead to nothing but extinction.

Toby Critchley (11)
Bishop Vesey's Grammar School, Sutton Coldfield

Bullying

To all the bullies out there
I know you probably don't care
What you are doing is traduce
So we have decided to produce
A saying to stop you all
From letting each other's hearts fall

Here it is
Are you ready for this?
Stop bullying!

Matthew Arnold (12)
Bishop Vesey's Grammar School, Sutton Coldfield

The Air We Breathe

Coughing, choking, spluttering
On the toxic gases in which we breathe
It's everywhere, no escape
From the invisible killer

It has stricken so many
Made them dead
But when will we learn
When to stop
Polluting the world we love?

Oliver Ho (11)
Bishop Vesey's Grammar School, Sutton Coldfield

Zena!

I remember Zena
Eyes aglow
Running in the snow
Leaping high, bringing a tear to my eye

I remember Zena
Lapping her drink
Making me blink
Running like the wind
Like a song you sing

I remember Zena
Sleeping on her bed
Dreams in her head
About a big dinner
Like a worthy winner

I remember Zena
Barking all night
Giving us a fright
I'm thinking of her now
To her, I take a bow

I remember Zena!

Amy Mumford (11)
Bishop Walsh Catholic School, Sutton Coldfield

Trapped

In all the world around me
The scene begins to slow
And suddenly, I am stopped
It seems I cannot go!

I am plunged into deep water
My breathing begins to falter
I attempt to scream and cry
Nobody can hear
All I smell is dampness and fear
Oh Lord, I think I am going to die

The world is closing in on me
My vision is flickering black and white
I have to hold my breath
Will I escape this feeling of death?
Yes, I must win the fight
And overcome this battle with anxiety

I close my eyes
Fire and ice
Is consuming my body
Echoing around
Voices can be found
Has help come for me?

I blink my eyes open
Oh my, I am so confused

I am on the ground
And I am shaking all around
This makes no sense at all

I look up and see that
A crowd is around me
Full of frightened stares
And disapproving glares
My mind clouds with the thought
Of wanting to escape reality

I grip my knees tightly
My hands are so sweaty and numb
The soles of my feet are throbbing
And my legs are weak with fear
When will the end of this event come?

People are attempting to calm me
There is a murmur drifting around
But all I hear
Is a crackling cacophony in my ears
Making my stomach twist and turn
I begin to heave
The sour taste of vomit captures my throat
Like a dry, scorching, hot burn

Then everything goes silent
The only sound is blood pounding in my ears
As I begin to enter a stable state

A delicate whisper as my guide
And a gentle hand
Wiping away my tears

I find myself in an empty corridor
With only a single person left standing there
A familiar girl, my friend, holding out her hand
I reach out and grasp it
Slowly standing up with caution
So my weak legs do not give way under me

As we walk on
Whilst I tuck in my shirt
And brush off my skirt
Ears blazing hot with embarrassment
She turns to me, smiling, then says
That what I just experienced
Was of something I have always dreaded
A panic attack
The anxiety had indeed
Messed with my head.

Molly Hughes (13)
Ounsdale High School, Wombourne

Poetry Escape - West Midland Poets

Wombourne

Around Wombourne there are many places to visit,
pubs and cafés that are filled with spirit.
There is Farmer and Friends and Coffee 212
there are also many other places to visit too.
Inside pubs, people enjoy their yummy food
while everyone's in a cheerful mood.

Cycling along the railway walk can be so much fun
and there are plenty of places to go for a run.
There are lots of lovely walks to take your dog
and a paddle in the brook in search of a frog.

At the leisure centre, you can do lots of sporty things,
at the music school you can play an instrument that has strings.
There are lots of sports activities to do, including swimming,
cricket and football,
while the church stands so very, very tall.

There are four primary schools which have many strict rules.
A very large secondary school
that has its own swimming pool.
Children come from far and wide,
to study hard and play outside.

Wombourne is a great place to come,
where you'll have so much fun.

William Tyne (12)
Ounsdale High School, Wombourne

My Dad Always Says

"So much has changed,"
my dad always says
"Since the day when I was a lad,
from the way we said hey
to computers, we'd play
to the vitamin D that we'd lack."

"You kids, these days,"
my dad always says
"You just don't know what you've got,
all of you moan
about things you don't own
'cause you can't see that you own the lot!"

"You have all these games,"
my dad always says
"You have smartphones and holidays and more,
but when you can't get your way
it's me that you blame
and in my face that you slam the door."

"When I was your age,"
my dad always says
"I didn't have the gifts that you've had,
I never went to watch Wolves
had the kits or the balls
but my childhood wasn't so bad."

"But some things won't change,"
my dad always says
"That's the love I have for my kids."
And he's sorry he moans when he hears us moan
See, the truth is, I know that he'd wish,
to give all that he has to see us both laugh,
to see us both smile in bliss
He would give the whole world to his boy and his girl
'cause we are his world's greatest gift
so my dad always says.

Kieran Lavender (12)
Ounsdale High School, Wombourne

Brexit - The Uncivil War

Were we to know that it would be such a sham?
Were we to know the effects of this uncivil scam?

The arguments that we have every day
As to whether we should stay or break away

Will the matter ever be settled?
Or will those young petals feel unsettled?

First, we had a plan A, and then a plan B
But with each passing day, the country continues to plea

With May and Corbyn at each other's throats
While the rest of parliament try to keep up and continue to take notes

Who should we support: Labour or Conservative?
Or do you think that both are just negative?

The continuous battle of slithering snakes
The continuous arguments for the same mistakes

We can see the fusillade of insults
And are hoping for positive results

While we count each passing hour
And see these people abuse their power

While so many of us live in fear about the future
The rest of us just watch their passing bloopers

Brexit, the uncivil war, the continuous was of thoughts and ideas,
The long-drawn physical, and emotional battles,
The lackadaisical and uninterested politicians

The moment that will go down in history, and the moment that could stop us from bouncing back

Is Brexit an uncivil war?

Josh Stevens (12)
Ounsdale High School, Wombourne

Today Is The Day

Today is the day I am to be wed
To the man I love, the man of my dreams
My future is about to be changed, forever
I am left alone in my dressing room and there is a knock
I see a woman at my door
She is walking in with my body, my face
Knife to my chest, I am trying to scream, it is too late
I collapse to the ground
I can feel the pain and now it goes again
Am I dead? Is this the end?
I won't rise
Can they not hear my screams?
Deafened must they be?
Blood is running but I don't rise
She has stolen my face, my body has the same scars
And my dress covered in blood, my blood
She is grabbing my bouquet and laughing at me
How terrible my fate is and how it has become
She is standing, dancing, grinning in the mirror
Mouthing the words 'I do'
She is walking up to me, eyes large, filled with horror
I can feel her breath on my cheeks
And she is whispering, "I'll take care of him."
I try to scream, "That should be me!"
She walks away and takes everything

My wedding, identity and life
I am left frozen. Alone. Lifeless.

Grace Hollington (12)
Ounsdale High School, Wombourne

My Seasons Poem

When spring arrives, daffodils bloom
And bluebells take up all the room
Birds chirping in their nests
Children eating Easter eggs
Farmers watching their cattle by night
Leaves blossom ever so bright

When summer arrives, there is no school
Time to jump in the swimming pool
Summer has some really long days
A perfect time for holidays
Time to play out with your friends
Quick! Have a barbecue, your summer fun will soon end

Shorter days and darker nights
Halloween fun and Bonfire Night
Orange, yellow, red and green
Leaves start falling off the trees
Days are grey, boring and old
Christmas decorations up, all silver and gold

Snow starts falling
And the church bells are calling
The trees are bare with nothing to show
And birds migrate in the winter snow
Everyone celebrate, everyone cheer
It's time to enjoy a happy new year!

Thomas Sidaway (13)
Ounsdale High School, Wombourne

Deep Waters

A young angel is calling from the deep waters tonight
But the water silences her and dims out her light
She longs for the life that has been taken away
So she continues to wait every night and day

A young angel is crying for the help of a friend
But they betrayed her and left her alone and abandoned
She now wishes that someone could hear her loud screams
So she remains there as nightmares replace her sweet dreams

A young angel is breaking as her memories fade
But no one can comfort her or remind her of her name
She has become more distant than an angel should be
So she waits in the ocean with a wish to be free

A young angel is drowning within her own fears
But the heaven's light won't take her, even if it appears
She still hopes one day she could redeem her wronged right
So she sits there calling from deep waters tonight.

Kayleigh Barnett-West (14)
Ounsdale High School, Wombourne

My Day At The Beach

I lie here on my sunbed
Gazing out at the deep blue sea
Feeling the red-hot sun
Blazing down on me

The light bouncing off the ocean
Breathing in the scent of suntan lotion
There is not a cloud in the sky
I sit back, deep in thought and sigh

Children playing with beachballs
Brightly coloured ice cream stalls
Palm trees swaying in the breeze
Stripy deck chairs put up with ease

Rainbow-coloured parasols dotted all around
Flip-flops kicked off on the ground
Running along the ocean shore
To the rockpools, where we will explore!

Lilos bobbing up and down
People come from out of town
Beach bags full to the brim
For the sun, sea, sand and to swim!

It's time to pack our things away
We hope to do this again someday

On the horizon, the sun starts to set
My day at the beach, I will never forget!

Lily May Morgan (12)
Ounsdale High School, Wombourne

Nanny's Heart

'A golden heart stopped beating
Hardworking hands at rest
It broke our hearts to see you go
But God only takes the best'

God...
Please tell her that we love her
And miss her every day
And tell her there's still so much
That we would like to say

We loved the nights we stayed at your house
But little did you know
We grabbed the biscuits from the pantry
And said, "Upstairs we go!"

We always talked into the night
While you were sound asleep
And when we could not doze off
You told us to count sheep

Our nanny is a love heart
That splits into six
That's the number of her grandchildren
Whose hearts will soon be fixed

So as we say goodbye today
We hope to see you one more time

God better take care of you
And feed you lots of wine!

Harriet Ann Humpherson (11)
Ounsdale High School, Wombourne

Emotions

Happiness is hard to find
Where love can make us blind
We all experience pain
but from it, power we gain

We drown in an ocean
of pain and emotion
Sadness, anxiety, happiness

We turn happy to sad
I am turning happy to sad
We turn loving to hating
I am turning loving to hating

We drown in an ocean
Of pain and emotion
Sadness, anxiety, happiness

Happiness is hard to find
We all experience pain
No matter how you feel, know I feel it too

Where love can make us blind
But from it, power we gain
No matter how you feel, know I feel it too

Pain, sadness, sorrow and regret
That's how I'm feeling

Happiness, hope, pride and satisfaction
That's how I should be feeling

Sadness... can stop
Anxiety... can stop
Love... is eternal.

Lauren Paige Hodgkins (12)
Ounsdale High School, Wombourne

Under The Sea

Take a trip down
Into the cerulean setting
As aqua bubbles ascend
Meet new marine friends!

The fish, the whales, the sharks
All see you and smile
The thalassic depths wave to you
This water is not hostile

The people don't drown
And the sharks don't attack
But suddenly, going deeper
Blue turns to black

The darkness consumes light
The pressure burdens
The life is gone
And you are lost...

But on the horizon!
A ray of light
It guides you
Even in this black of night

An angler fish becomes an angelfish
By illuminating a path

You see the safety of the surface
As you escape the ocean's wrath

But is the land much purer
Than sharks that bite?
Or is the very place we live
Darker than the darkest night?

Mark Cox (14)
Ounsdale High School, Wombourne

My Tree

There it is, tall and powerful
'My tree'
Standing still, waiting for me
Head high, and proud
All its secrets in the ground

For years 'my tree'
Has watched life go by
Saw young soldiers, fly planes in the sky
Then heard their young widows
Beneath your branches cry
Keeping their secrets in the ground

How many children
Have climbed your boughs
And fallen to the ground?
Your soil soaked up all their tears
Your leaves soothed their fears
Then you 'kept' their secrets
in the ground

'My tree'
What do you see
When you look at me?
Who, what will I be?
You watch me grow
Knowing one day I will go

Out into the world
And I know
You will keep my secrets
In the ground.

Terrell Bennett (14)
Ounsdale High School, Wombourne

Blue

Blue is a colour that represents many of the things that we all do with glee
Like going on holiday and swimming in the sea
Blue is a colour that represents water
It is what I am drinking now, sat here as an author
Blue is a colour that represents the cold
So go outside and create a memory you can hold
Blue is a colour that makes up a rainbow
You might see one if you look out of the window
Blue is a colour that can be part of the moon
There might be one tomorrow, at 12 noon
Blue is a colour that represents the ocean
If you are going to swim in it, use some sun lotion
Blue is a colour that represents the sky
So go on a plane and fly up high
Blue is a colour that represents peace
So take a moment to think what it would be like
If it was like that on all of the streets.

Joe Conway-Lees (12)
Ounsdale High School, Wombourne

Things To Do

In the UK, there is lots to do
Watching YouTube or having fun
Going to town with your friends
Having a sleepover, *fun, fun, fun*

In Jersey, there is lots to do
On the beach or in the café
Fish and chips and meatballs
Their creamy ice cream is the best
In the countryside, how about that
Or relaxing in the sun on the golden beach
Getting that tan, there is nothing better

In America, there is lots to do
In Disneyland or at the zoo
Playing with your friends, what could be better?
Having fun with lots of laughter

Then there is good old Wales
Rain, rain, rain, what fun!
Staying indoors, there is nothing better
Going shopping for winter clothes
Heating turned up all of the year
No hot sun, it's freezing cold.

James Price (12)
Ounsdale High School, Wombourne

Our Anxiety

We can't ask how your day was
We can't ask if we can have more food
Without having the fear of getting it wrong and being
Stupid or getting it right and being a know-it-all
Who understands?

"Just relax."
"Just calm down."
"Take a chill pill."
"Stop over exaggerating."
"Just ignore it."
"It's all in your head."
A black cloud is following us
Fear
We start crying
We feel
Weak
We tell someone they don't understand
For every
Tear
We shed a second of our future is
Lost

The black cloud follows, taking over us
Thought by thought
Fear controls us
Anxiety controls us

Who understands?
Who listens?

Niamh Carrothers (13)
Ounsdale High School, Wombourne

The English Seaside

A gentle breeze, waves breaking on the shore
Early morning walkers, dogs running in the sand
Beachcombers, kicking driftwood, looking for creatures afar
The start of another day at the English seaside

Sand dunes and rockpools, deckchairs, windbreaks
Bouncing beachballs, buckets and spades
Ice-cold drinks and an aroma of fish and chips
Covered in suncream, children playing, laughing and crying
Adults sleeping, seagulls squawking on another day at the English seaside

The last few surfers still wait for the perfect wave
The sun begins to set
The shutters come down
Day-trippers are gone
The only sound that's heard are amusement arcades
Until dusk becomes dawn
This is the end of another perfect day at the English seaside.

Amelia Rowsell (12)
Ounsdale High School, Wombourne

A Friend

To my friend, Reece

A friend is someone you can laugh with
A friend is someone you can play games with
A friend is someone you can spend time with
A friend is someone you can go online with

But what about when you are sad
And when life is hard
If you need to get things off your chest
That is the true friendship test

When you need someone to count on
To get you through the bad times
When life seems like it's going wrong
I will stand by you and we will be strong

A friend is someone that listens
A friend is a shoulder to cry on
A friend is there every step of the way
A friend is there for you each and every day

From now until you're on the mend
I promise you, I will be your best friend.

Kaiden Sidaway (12)
Ounsdale High School, Wombourne

The Boy Of Mystery

Through the air, this person flies by
A mysterious world before our eyes
Not content to be just a human being
A person with powers you have never seen

A secret world of shadows and magic
Created by loved ones whose death was tragic

Snake-like features will come to appear
Whenever evil is close and near
From a baby's tear, a scar appeared
Laid next to his mother who then disappeared

A unique orphan this child became
Whose care from relatives meant life would never be the same

Out of sadness, a new, adventure was born
His journey was magical but was sometimes torn

Can you guess? Are your conclusions hotter?
Yes indeed, it's Mr Harry Potter.

Suzie Aston (13)
Ounsdale High School, Wombourne

Excitement

I am the adorable fluffy puppy you've been waiting for
I am the fantastic £1,000 million pounds you've just won
I am the proud parent of the healthy, soft-skinned newborn baby
I am the glistening diamond ring given to you by your loving fiancé
I am the pair of designer high-heeled shoes you have just bought
I am the luxurious foreign holiday you've just booked
I am the captivated child being entertained by the clumsy, silly clown at a birthday party
I am the confident, graceful dancer performing on the stage
I am the child waiting with anticipation to see if Santa has been on Christmas morning
I am the football fan nervously watching their team playing in the cup final
I am excitement!

Caitlyn Douch (14)
Ounsdale High School, Wombourne

The World, Our Home

The world is such a wonderful place
However, we are such a disgrace
The battered and bruised ocean is crying
The vulnerable world is slowly dying

The world is such a wonderful place
However, we are such a disgrace
We need to stop dumping our waste
But let's fix the world with our paste

The world is such a wonderful place
However, we are such a disgrace
We need to *stop* deforestation
Our kind is an abomination

The world is such a wonderful place
But we are such a disgrace
The level of pollution in the air is rising
The world is slowly dying

Do your job to protect the world
So get up and fix your mistakes...

Evie Hollington (11)
Ounsdale High School, Wombourne

The Football Fright

This game will give you quite a thrill
In summer's heat or autumn's chill
Popping pads and pouncing feet
Will lead to our opponents' defeat
A taste of sweet, hit after hit
The offence and defence never quit
Move the ball and stop the run
Let's show the fans who's number one

As we walk on the field
Band playing, the crowd roaring
Fans on the field for a run-through
Mist of smoke in the tunnel
You can't replace the feeling with anything
Stomach and can't breathe
Bands start playing, we run out, slapping hands
The lights are bright, you can only see the field
And the team get ready to win the game.

Jack Lloyd (11)
Ounsdale High School, Wombourne

Freedom

An opening door
A distance away from that bitter sore
A shine of light
A feeling that feels so right

Out of your nightmarish chains
Like a horse cut through from his reins
Freedom isn't always when you're awake
It's just a break from that spiteful ache

A ring of a bell
Words you can finally tell
The feeling of peace
A time to release

Gaining independence
A feeling of brilliance
A bird being let out of his cage
An end to your outrage

Freedom to take a hike
Freedom to do things you like
Your short journey of fun
This is freedom.

Halle Glover (12)
Ounsdale High School, Wombourne

Snow Days

Cold wind rushing through the air
Snow lies on the ground
Covering all to see
Absorbing all the sound

Ice crystals glistening
Like stars in the midnight sky
Delicate snowflakes dancing
Fluttering from way up high

Iridescent icicles
Sitting on each house
When walking down the street
It is as quiet as a mouse

Trees with only branches
Turned white from the frost
Beneath the soft white blanket
Autumn leaves are lost

Sledging down the hillside
"One... two... three... let's go!"
Everybody laughing
Winter's better with snow.

Emily Roberts (12)
Ounsdale High School, Wombourne

Seasons Of The Year

Spring, the start of the year
A season where life blossoms
Where the atmosphere is clear
This is a great time of year

In summer, the heat is blistering
The ground becomes parched
Everybody and everything is sweltering
The water, once fresh, now becomes scorched

Autumn, the time where temperature cools
The shedding of leaves from deciduous trees
Where the ground soon fills with miniature pools
And everything from plants to bees starts to freeze

The last season of the year
Winter, the coldest season
The shortest day and longest night
No one even knows its reason.

Noah Bradburn (13)
Ounsdale High School, Wombourne

Alone...

I found myself alone
The anxious butterflies fluttered within

What I hate about her -
She is a tyrant!
I care, share, help and listen
Yet, she sniggers, humiliates and stares
Supposing herself superior
Why don't you leave me alone?

What I hate about her -
She is slippery!

She has slippery scales along her back
Her forked tongue is dishonest
Carelessly, she calls harsh names
Why don't you leave me alone?

I found myself alone, but no longer
I stood on my own two feet

What I love about me -
I am victorious!

Mia White (14)
Ounsdale High School, Wombourne

Cats

They have gentle eyes that see so much
Paws that have the silent touch
Purrs to signal 'all is okay'
And cats show more love than exceptional words can tell
Elegant movements touched with honour
A soothing companionship by our side
A friendship that takes time to bloom
Small wonder why we love them so much
As I go through my long school day
Expectations on me
My BFF is always there when I get home
To calm my troubled mind
My friend is very special
He has a truly amazing soul
He's velvety and gentle
For he's my cat, after all.

Eva Bradburn (12)
Ounsdale High School, Wombourne

Is This Reality Now?

How many people were stabbed this week?
Did they find who did it?
Do the elderly feel safe going to the shops?
Is it a shock when you hear the sirens?
What words do they speak?

I cannot say it's become normalised now
Will it ever?
The elderly, would you feel safe walking past gangs
Late at night, staring at you as you pass?
Or would your heart race as you look at the floor
and walk a little faster?
No, even young ears are used to it as the blue flashing lights
move out of vision
Were they words? Or just jumbled letters, given a meaning?

Charlotte Phillips (15)
Ounsdale High School, Wombourne

Snow

We watch as snow falls out of the sky
As it settles on the ground
It can be predicted
We can prepare
We'll sit and watch the grit trucks
But we act so unaware

Children welcome it gleefully
Praying to miss school
Wanting to make a snowman
Wishing for more
Ignoring the cold temperatures
Only watching the snow-covered floor

Trains and buses get cancelled
Further delaying adults
Creating a whirlpool of despair
As people slip and slide
As they try not to fall
They attempt to glide
Only to fall further behind.

Lillie Ann Perry (13)
Ounsdale High School, Wombourne

Death Rose

There it is, the crime is done
The last petal on the rose has gone
The murderer has been found
And the murdered, ten foot in the ground

The face of his victim's flush
The lips, their souls blue
His success to their fall
Came a great depression to all

Victor Floyd was his name
And sorrow followed wherever he became
But now he's on death row
Death by hanging is how he goes

A new rose grows from the ash
Hopefully not as bad as the last
The murderer has been found
And the murderer is ten foot in the ground.

Joshua Riley Thompson (12)
Ounsdale High School, Wombourne

The Fight Of The Mirror Carp

As I sit there with the gentle wind in my face
The rippling water carries my fluorescent float off
in anticipation of a catch

As the corn and maggots sink calmly to the bottom
an unexpected fish seize their prey

Strike! I feel the power and tension at the end of the line
What could this humongous beast be on the end?
The fish tugging and pulling the line on the curved rod
As I reel this gigantic fish in, I can see its beautiful scales,
Its eyes dazzling in the light and the textured fins
It is a mirror carp!

Ethan Lamsdale (11)
Ounsdale High School, Wombourne

Emotions

Sad is a baby blue
It tastes like a burning mint in your mouth
Makes you personally feel blue
Rain from your eyes
It feels like a bomb travelling down your throat
Reminding us that life has curious emotions

Happiness is a bright yellow sun
It tastes like yummy, sweet candy
Like you are a shining sun in the sky
Screams, cheers and laughter from your mouth
It smells like a summer's day: flowers, sun and grass
It sounds like a chuckling kookaburra
Happiness takes you to a spectacular, beautiful world.

Megan Tune (12)
Ounsdale High School, Wombourne

Differences

Roses are red
Violets are blue
We all have differences, just like you
No matter who or where you are
You'll always have a place in someone's heart
Sugar is sweet and so are you
Ignore what the haters say
And love your life day to day
You know how I mentioned blue?
Well here is another part of the poem for you
Blue is where the sky and the sea meet
It is often used for depth and stability
It symbolises your trust, loyalty
Wisdom and more, like confidence, intelligence
And your love for all.

Nikita Crooke (12)
Ounsdale High School, Wombourne

Sharks

Greetings sharks, to explore the
ocean, grey, white hammer
nurse, whale, reef, bull, all
are large and all are full -
fresh meat inside, they are
content

Swish, swosh, dive, they move with
speed and aggression, there is no
affection in the shark, their bark
is certainly frightful and dark

Swim, swim, can you hide or will
you be caught inside, inside those
huge and scary jaws? There is
no pause, for the predator or
the ocean there is always
a commotion.

Layla Causer (12)
Ounsdale High School, Wombourne

A Spectrum Of Emotions

A whirlwind of emotion
A thunderstorm of conflict
An ocean of the mind

To speak or to suffer
To confess or regret
To love or to hate

To think or to sink
To laugh or to cry
To reveal or conceal

Anger like a hurricane
Sadness like a storm and
Joy like the sun

A blanket of terror
A blizzard of fury
A black hole of regret

Confusion
Hate and
Passion

The mind
The fun
The horror
And the love.

Joshua Edward Sanderson (11)
Ounsdale High School, Wombourne

You Are Beautiful

You are beautiful
You don't know
How lovely
You are
You know exactly
What you want and
Who you want to be
You don't have to change a thing
The world should change itself
Your body being different
Doesn't make you ugly!
It makes you unique and special
The people that make fun of you
Just for being different
Are jealous because they know
They will never be as beautiful as you!
You are capable of amazing things
Never forget that.

Emelia Grace Edwards (12)
Ounsdale High School, Wombourne

Pollution

Everywhere I go, I see pollution
It scares me every day
I wonder what the world will become
If all we do is abuse it?

Pollution is something we increase every day
Trying to get to work faster, shop faster
Little do we know it is bad
Little do we know we are in danger
If we don't stop it

Things used to be so good
Walking and biking everywhere we travelled
I wish we would treat this world with respect
and hopefully not ruin it for all.

Eve Lewis (13)
Ounsdale High School, Wombourne

Perfect

She's got one million likes
I wouldn't even get one
She looks perfect
My hair isn't even done

She's beach body ready
I'm really not
She has perfect skin
All I have are spots

But her photos don't show everything
They don't show her struggles
They don't show her alone
With all of her troubles

My life may not be perfect
But I suppose it is okay
I mean, who wants to be perfect anyway?

Emily Crump (15)
Ounsdale High School, Wombourne

Snow

The cold, the rain
Falling as snow
Softly landing
On the ground
Crisp and white
Waiting for footprints
To make a crunching sound

Pure white snow
Crispy and sparkly
Every flake is different
Every flake is unique
So catch one on your tongue and let it melt

Crisp, cold, white
Falling from the sky
Crisp, cold, white
Soon we'll say goodbye
Goodbye to the glisten...
Goodbye to the white...

Jennie Louisa Stevens (12)
Ounsdale High School, Wombourne

Life With Anxiety

Life with anxiety
Life with anxiety gives you stress
Life with anxiety is not a blessing
Even though your mind is telling you
something that you know is not true
Your mind will work overtime
making you feel blue
It makes you feel worried and sad
but in all fairness
it may not be that bad...
There are many places you can get help
Then you will not feel trapped in the cell of anxiety
If you suffer, please speak out!

Willow Brittle (14)
Ounsdale High School, Wombourne

My Happy Place

When I feel sad or angry or upset
I go to my happy place
I lie on my bed and close my eyes
And think about bright blue skies
I breathe slowly like the breeze
And picture lots of fuzzy bees
I stroke the silky duvet cover
And imagine blossom trees with birds that hover
I feel relaxed, calm and peaceful
And think about flowery fields
I feel my pillow against my head
And come back to reality where I'm lying in bed.

Lily Collins (11)
Ounsdale High School, Wombourne

Football

F ans cheering wildly, excited about the game
O h no! We're losing already?
O ffside? The linesman has decided and the crowd groans
T op of the league is where we want to be
B ottom of the league is not an option
A fan invades the pitch, everyone roars and complains
L aughter and cheers are heard all around as the match plays on
L ong live football, the best game in the world!

Tom Priest (12)
Ounsdale High School, Wombourne

A Spring Day

Seeds from dandelions flutter frivolously overhead
Snowdrops as white as a glacier waiting patiently for spring to dance
The powerful wind chases the sweet smell of lavender and it swirls like a scarf
Nettles and thorns wait viciously to harm any innocents as they pass by
In a flash, rain pours down like a waterfall - drenching one to the core
Puddles so deep - reflecting a deep blue, optimistic sky
The heavens close
Silence...

Sophia Grinsell (12)
Ounsdale High School, Wombourne

Little Robin

I look outside my window to see
A little robin nesting in a tree
Oh, how beautiful he looks
Just like the pictures in the books
Off you go, flying freely in the snow
As you land so gracefully
You look around so hastily
Searching for young
While you tweet a little song
Grabbing your food so tight
While you fly in the night
Finally, you're back where you belong in your house
Where nothing goes wrong.

Kyla Williams (12)
Ounsdale High School, Wombourne

The Running River

Blue liquids run, looking for destiny
Crashing into rocks roughly

The beautiful creatures leap and dance in the water
Boats sail along as the fishermen battle
The hook sinks to the bed of the river
A poor, majestic creature takes a bite
And now it's dinner!

Finally, they stop for the night
The day has grown old and the river finally meets its destination
But the endless cycle carries on...

Daniel Lowe (12)
Ounsdale High School, Wombourne

Reflection

I sat and stared at the blinding white
Discarded emotion all around
Tick-tock goes the clock
Waiting for the colours to walk in

Ideas come and go
But a portrait sticks to mind
The eyes, nose and mouth
A million ways to make them come alive

The water fills with ripples
As the paint adds its colour
The brush strokes the ice-white paper
Now, my reflection is complete.

Molly Rebecca Rabone (12)
Ounsdale High School, Wombourne

Friends

They're there to cheer you up,
and also to say, "What's up?"
So when you're feeling down,
they turn that frown upside down.
Friends help you along the way when you,
don't know what to say,
and always have your back,
even when you slack.

Don't take them for granted,
even if you're sad or mad.
'Cause they might even find you,
a good-looking lad!

Lottie May Beardsmore (11)
Ounsdale High School, Wombourne

The Mysterious Night Boy

Inspired by 'At Algeciras - A Meditation Upon Death'

In the rich midnight of the garden trees
Till dawn breaks upon those mingled seas
The big, bright, powerful moon shone onto the land
As it chased the darkness, the fears away
A shadow with nobody curiously came towards me
He greeted me with pixie dust, just enough for two
His eyes, so brown, so kind but... a hint of evil
But you could clearly see that he wasn't the devil
He slowly took my frightened hand
and now we are in Neverland
Laughing and cheering, protecting ourselves
Why, when no harm can be done while you're together
He was the one who taught me how to fight
I will protect him always and with all my might
I have created strong feelings for him, a way I never felt
Why do I feel this way?
But still, his heart is grey
He sees my feelings for him, I can't hide anything
He is the ruler of my heart and soul, he is my king
I know that we will be together forever, no matter what
We are so strong because our love will never be forgot
Together, we will rule Neverland.

Julia Piechaczek (12)
Our Lady & St Chad Catholic Academy, Wolverhampton

A Hungry Fox

I saw the sly old fox
Creep up to the chicken box
He sniffed and sniffed in the air
For he wanted to find a chicken there

But no chicken could be found
So he went and turned around
Went off in an unhappy mood
Searching for his midnight food.

Bethany Walker (12)
Ounsdale High School, Wombourne

Elephant

Save the elephant, proud and noble beast
Don't let the poachers on its ivory feast
Save the elephants, don't let them die
Don't let the children ask us why
When once, there were so many
But now, there are so few
Because I didn't do anything
Did you?

Millie Grace Taylor (12)
Ounsdale High School, Wombourne

Wolf

The wisp of the wind blows on my silver, silky fur
My eyes light up like a full moon
My ears hear every single sound
If you meet me, you meet your doom
At night I prowl around
The strength of me is in my pack
My claws as sharp as a razor blade
I am always ready for attack.

Millie Georgina Smart (11)
Ounsdale High School, Wombourne

Dreams

Every night, you have a dream
When you wake, they are not what they seem
Close your eyes and drift to sleep
Your dreams are yours and yours to keep
When you're visited by the man of sand
Drift away in a distant land
Sometimes magical, sometimes scary
There was even one where I followed a fairy.

Eden Randhawa (12)
Ounsdale High School, Wombourne

Lions

Big bushy manes
Bright orange
Like a sunset

Eating his lunch
Watch out, next it might be you
Wandering around outside his mansion

Glaring at you
With his large green eyes
Staring into space

Treading towards you
His steps get bigger
Coming to you for tea.

Rooooar!

Louise Walton (12)
Ounsdale High School, Wombourne

What A Smile He Had

What a smile he had
Even though he was sad
What a name
Such a shame

Always glad
He was a lad
Very bad
Always mad

He had a dad
Who was very mad
He had a mum
Who loved to drink rum

Lived in a big home
Who was always alone
His heart was one big stone
Nothing could break his bones.

Harley Brook Trow (14)
Ounsdale High School, Wombourne

My Four-Month-Old Brother Called Niran

I have a little brother,
We share the same mother.

I wouldn't trade him for another,
Even though he can be a little b*****

I walk him around the house
Like a lost little mouse

Whenever I'm feeling down
He turns my frown around

We share affection for one another
Because we share the same mother.

Tyrahan Singh Sandhu (12)
Ounsdale High School, Wombourne

The Starry Night

All was quiet
All was dark
In the burrow
Lived a tiny creature
With spiky spikes
Blinked with his eyes
In the starry night
The tiny creature
Was frightened and scared
Jumped out of the burrow
And ran into the grass
The tiny creature stared in the night
The tiny creature's eyes
Staring into the starry night.

Keira Davies (12)
Ounsdale High School, Wombourne

You Are Like...

You are like a shooting star
You can cross limits that reach so far
Like an angel shining so bright
Brave as a warrior and as mighty as a knight
A king, I could say, but you always have time to play
And by play, I mean stay
Because you're always here inside and out...

You are like a shooting star
You can cross limits that reach so far.

Michaella Tiniozou (12)
Ounsdale High School, Wombourne

Computer Game

F rom the Battle Bus, I jump
O ut comes my feathered flyer, gliding to the ground
R eady to battle to the win
T ilted Towers I go, ducking and hiding from opponents
N oobs are walking about in the open, bound to get shot
I build up and place my launch pad, off to the circle I go
T hink I may win the game
E ndgame is here, I've survived.

Daniel Jevons (12)
Ounsdale High School, Wombourne

Being Free

Flying above the white mists of the clouds
And over the blue abyss of the sea
Vast views of different homes
This is how it feels to be free

Look beneath me and see
The black void of scaly skin
Right behind is a snaking tail
A body of obsidian

A ground-shaking roar
A furious flame
Leaps across the sky
Like molten rain

That's what it's like to fly.

Alfie Thistle (12)
Ounsdale High School, Wombourne

Young Writers Information

We hope you have enjoyed reading this book – and that you will continue to in the coming years.

If you're a young writer who enjoys reading and creative writing, or the parent of an enthusiastic poet or story writer, do visit our website www.youngwriters.co.uk. Here you will find free competitions, workshops and games, as well as recommended reads, a poetry glossary and our blog. There's lots to keep budding writers motivated to write!

If you would like to order further copies of this book, or any of our other titles, then please give us a call or visit www.youngwriters.co.uk.

Young Writers
Remus House
Coltsfoot Drive
Peterborough
PE2 9BF
(01733) 890066
info@youngwriters.co.uk

Join in the conversation!
Tips, news, giveaways and much more!

YoungWritersUK   @YoungWritersCW

But to reject these cries for respect
Is blissful ignorance.

Maia Winter (17)
The Sixth Form College, Solihull

Infuriating, Isn't It?

We have the vote, we have our rights
So why? Why are we complaining?
Protesting, challenging, demanding
To be ignored

Does this infuriate you
All this whining and fuss
Even though her hand in marriage
Is forced at just twelve years old?

Even though, across the globe
She is sold as if an object
Trafficked, abused and exploited
A life destroyed

And then back home
She is treated as if an object
Jeering abuse, whistling in the street
So avoids walking alone

She sticks to her strengths
Looking beautiful and staying composed
Ensuring her skirt is just the right length
Fearing the consequences

Indeed, we have come so far
One hundred years of progress

Or makes it clear to understand
So the invasion shouldn't last as long as you speak
But there are those who can't form the sentence
Can anyone ever see or hear the depression?

Sophie Barnett (16)
The Sixth Form College, Solihull

Only Inside

Bright long hair that flows in the wind
Just an average child, they say, she is no different
As this bright long hair seems the only sore thumb
Standing out from any other features given
For that was only on the outside, like everything else
Just like her expressions and mannerisms, just listen
Did you ever feel emotions in secret?

Confused and wondering what feelings lie so deep
It tells you all never to stop and speak
Your parents or carers and even friends
Never know the alien invaded because it's hidden as a friend
But thinking too much, even in your sleep
Keeps your brain dancing with same old things
Did you ever hide from the monster in your dreams?

When the world seems bigger as you grow smaller
The alien inside hits a little stronger
Teardrops trickle like a fork in the river
Hopelessness tells you you're never forgiven
Sat all alone, believing it's deserving, you mark yourself
To remind you of the hurting
Did you ever hurt and speak out, feeling certain?

Some are too young and don't know to ask
But help is not always there without talking about the past
Not all education names the alien inside

And now, not a beacon of light to be clutched
It truly has lost all of its might
It's just the way it goes
That's what they told him

No heartbreak can compare to watching your home erupt in flames
Seeing all of the memories slowly fade and fade
To the invaders, this is all just fun and games
So they just sat and prayed and prayed
A childhood is quickly forgotten
As is the feeling of warmth and security
All that is left is ash and wood that is rotten
Now their souls have lost all purity
No heartbreak can compare to watching your home erupt in flames
That's what they forgot to tell him.

Melissa Allen (17)
The Sixth Form College, Solihull

The Effects Of War

The cold mistress of the night sneaks into the soldier's bed
Where he is turning and tossing and tossing and turning
All thoughts of peace lost and instead replaced with dread
Now his body is replaced with a deadly burning
It's the memories of war brandishing his skin
That keeps him awake at night
Reminding him of his deadly sin
Pull yourself together and fight
That's what they told him

There is no sound worse than a child's cry of agony
The sheer tormented terror -
Produced from a body so bony
How did we miss this error?
Naked in the streets, they run
Screaming for their mothers and
Trying to get out of range of the deadly shotgun
But they fail and limp bodies drop into the sand
There is no sound worse than a child's cry of agony
That's what they forgot to tell him

Long-limbed trees sway in the wind
Crying at seeing their fellow comrades fall
Now lying, barren and skinned
Whilst the fire continues to sing and dance and maul
Not a blade of grass is left untouched
A once illustrious sight

in the game of society,
they have been fooled,
they are angry - provoked,
cross, confused,
they call her names,
she falls again,
lost - enough,
but she tries again.

Emily Taylor (13)
The Coleshill School, Coleshill

The Truth

How can she stand,
skin so fair,
porcelain hands,
flowing hair,
ocean eyes,
gleaming smile,
full red lips,
flawless style?

But when you look,
inside her soul,
sorrow and fear,
an evil ghoul,
opinions - hard words,
they have sunk,
clasped tight,
judgement - thoughts,
hugging tighter than tight.

Further, she falls,
a harsh decline,
her eyes reflect,
her inner mind,
her darkened skin,
her reddened face,
from all the effort,
of trying to place,

Trance

Useless but easily manipulative saying words that do not mean anything.
Still, people fall into stupidity, not listening carefully or closely.
Draw these aliens, minions and hypnotised victims
of the poisonous letters away from the page - digitalised, I figure.
Even if they are bothered to use the lead, easily available, it still turns out dead.
The lead is terrible in flavour, but every now and then
I think to myself, *when will meaning be born again to help save the hole*
that only grows bigger in society's tastes that has become so bitter?

Angus Glover (14)
The Coleshill School, Coleshill

Racism Poetry

Being black
Does not decide my heart
Being brown
Does not make up my mind
Being white
Does not determine who I am inside
Do not be surprised when you see
That I don't let the colour of my skin determine me for who I am.
For who I am
Is who I decide to be.

Serena Nunda (12)
St Francis Of Assisi Catholic Technology College, Aldridge

Peace

P eople class peace as harmony and happiness
E ven though sometimes peace seems a lot to ask for
A sking for peace is easier than you think
C alm surroundings are the equivalent of peace
E vil should be banished for peace to grow.

Callum O'Brien (12)
St Francis Of Assisi Catholic Technology College, Aldridge

My Little Brother

My little brother, cute as can be
My little brother sings with glee
My little brother with light golden hair
Scares me out with a big, massive stare
My little brother, who looks like me
No one else is as clever as he
My little brother, I watch him go
My little brother, I love him so.

Eireann Mae Brannigan (12)
St Francis Of Assisi Catholic Technology College, Aldridge

Gymnastics Poem

The training lasts for moments
Though you can get hurt
It isn't all about the winning that counts
It is about hard work
The applause will never be forgotten
The prize will be kept
The long hours will never be a waste
In trying to win, you build a skill
You learn you can always do it.

Kelsey Leigh Harrison (12)
St Francis Of Assisi Catholic Technology College, Aldridge

School

S illy school, it's a horrible place
C hildren rushing there every day
H ow many days we waste there a year
O h, it's all about education, they say
O h, really, no one cares
L earning, learning all the time, it's just so boring and half of it we just forget!

Freya Coyne (12)
St Francis Of Assisi Catholic Technology College, Aldridge

Poem About Positivity

Always try your best
But give yourself a rest
Don't give up
It's not just luck
Just because you feel low
Doesn't mean you can't try
Even if at first, you don't succeed
Always know it's not just need
You should never give in
But know it's not the end
Positivity is the key.

Erin Brown (11)
St Francis Of Assisi Catholic Technology College, Aldridge

As The Ice Begins To Melt

All the wonderful polar bears
Hunt like tigers
They all see something
But don't care a bit
They gaze upon the weather
It seems that it has changed
As the ice begins to melt
They all begin to compress
Before they all fall
Into the cold, cold water
Please pray for them!
So it won't happen again.

Aleksandra Chelchowska (12)
St Francis Of Assisi Catholic Technology College, Aldridge

We Are All The Same

It does not matter about our skin
We are all still the same
They are no different because of their colour
They are no better or worse
So stop being racist because of their colour

There are different ways to be racist
Bullying because of their colour or race
But we should not do it at all because we are all the same.

Ashton Jones (11)
St Francis Of Assisi Catholic Technology College, Aldridge

Bullies, Bullies, Go Away

Swinging punches
Screaming names
Telling lies about my shame
All because of a silly game

Crying in the corner
All upset
Knowing that my name was said
Tears falling down my face

I hope they don't find my hiding place
Away in the shed
Screaming names, swinging punches
Bullies, bullies, go away!

Louise Kent (12)
St Francis Of Assisi Catholic Technology College, Aldridge

Shark Eyes!

While I was swimming in the sea
I saw a great white shark glaring at me
Looking deep into my eyes
I knew he was wise!
When my gaze met his and his met mine
It seemed as if we were lost in time
And as we lingered in our stare
I could find no malice there
What I saw was the life within
As he studied me and I studied him...

Abigail Brookes (11)
St Francis Of Assisi Catholic Technology College, Aldridge

Balloons

Friends are like balloons that you love
If you let them go, they will fly above
Keep them close and never let go
Then have fun and let the time flow
Friends are like balloons because they stick together
Friends are like balloons because they will be friends forever
Friends are bulletproof
And you have nothing to lose
Far away, far away!

Charlotte Freeth (12)
St Francis Of Assisi Catholic Technology College, Aldridge

The Tiger's Poem

With its enormous paws
And fearful claws

Black and orange stripes seen for miles
Its prey's dead corpse left in piles

Teeth, sharp as blades
Bones used for trades

Its body sold at markets
Skin used as carpets

Almost wiped off the planet
Many countries trying to ban it

This is the poem of the roaring tiger!

Erin Feely (12)
St Francis Of Assisi Catholic Technology College, Aldridge

Futures

On the news
Another life lost
Another future gone
All because of a knife

Will you think
Before you pick up a knife?
More youngsters at risk
Because of your knife

Families mourn
Because of you
Just because you've
Picked up that knife

Dreams destroyed
Because of you
Big dreams lost
Part of the cost.

Ryan Richards (13)
St Francis Of Assisi Catholic Technology College, Aldridge

Pollution

Cars rush by, black smoke flies
Sweet wrappers and bottles fall to the ground
Things like waste get dumped into the now green-looking river
Black smoke billows out of the power plant
The ice in the north is melting; polar bears are losing their homes
Trees are falling down with a pound and a snap, birds' eggs crack and don't live
What have we done to this world?

Matthew John Logan (12)
St Francis Of Assisi Catholic Technology College, Aldridge

War Poem - When Will This End?

My life is filled with ruins
most of them I grew up in
the sound of the bombs
and the sound of kids losing their moms

I see dead bodies beneath the rubble
and the slanted walls that crumble
I try to fill my head with joy
with the smell of cakes and sweets galore

I smell the earth burning away
and the smell of bodies decaying
I hear the bombs and the guns
oh, please make it stop!

Shantel Odera Dike (12)
St Francis Of Assisi Catholic Technology College, Aldridge

Don't Do It

D on't do it
O ne day, it may happen to you
N ot being a bully is important
T hey may be hurt by your actions

B ullying is wrong
E ven bullies are hurt by other bullies

A re you hurting them inside?

B eing bullied hurts
U nderstand how others feel
L isten to yourself
L isten to others
Y ou wouldn't like to be bullied.

Harvey Williams-Castle (12)
St Francis Of Assisi Catholic Technology College, Aldridge

Poem About Bullying

Words can hurt, can make me cry
My tears coming from the sky
The words that you say upset me
Why can't you just leave me be?

Words can hurt, can make me cry
My tears coming from the sky
You bully me and my friends to look cool
Don't you know that you're just a big fool

Words can hurt, can make me cry
My tears coming from the sky
Sometimes, words can hurt me the most
It makes me feel like a ghost.

Sean Andrew Florence (12)
St Francis Of Assisi Catholic Technology College, Aldridge

War!

When day becomes night, the soldiers still fight
Fighting for their dignity
Fighting for their homes and families
When residents have no choice but to leave their homes
Leave families to become refugees
Young and old
Waking up to, not alarms, but the flashes of bright red and orange lights
The loud, ear-piercing screams of the gunshots right outside their doors
Young and old
Being rushed to the hospital because of this series of torturous events.

Holly Christine Mountford (12)
St Francis Of Assisi Catholic Technology College, Aldridge

Rainy Days

Raindrops fall
Drip! Drop!
Time to put on my wellies and go outside

Splish! Splosh!
Jumping in puddles
Leaving an almighty mess

The amount of rain was the same as an infinity pool
Water seeping through my clothes
Wonder if there will be that pot of gold that will bring me luck?

A rainbow starts to break through
My wishes have come true!
Happiness is all around me
Now the pot of gold has found me!

Amelia Williams (12)
St Francis Of Assisi Catholic Technology College, Aldridge

My Sister, Leah

She might be different
She might stand out
I feel so sad
People look and stare
I feel so bad
It makes me wonder
It makes me think
So what if she is different?
So what if she stands out?
After all
She is my sister
She can stand out
She is my little girl
My little princess
Say something to her and I'll be there
Don't hurt my sister, please
She is my life
I love you to the moon and back
Always have
And always will.

Gabby Nolan (11)
St Francis Of Assisi Catholic Technology College, Aldridge

Our Green Planet

Our green planet
Is suffering at our hands
And the blame can be placed
Firmly on man

Rainforests dwindling
Waiting for their demise
Nature watches in horror
As the animal kingdom cries

Landfills are increasing
People are slow to change their ways
Greenhouse gases fill the air
It's numbering our days

We have to change our mindset
Reduce, recycle, reuse
You can help us save our Earth
Go out, change people's views!

Míceál Duggan-Wadehra (12)
St Francis Of Assisi Catholic Technology College, Aldridge

Broken Voices

Everything around you is still
Everything around you shatters
You curl up in a ball
Hoping you will heal, but none of that matters
Because no one can hear your cry
Your voice is broken, it's too late to try

You finally open yourself up like a book
After being held hostage by your silence
You gulp down your fear and seek help because it is never too late
You shouldn't give up and let them knock you down
As if you were nothing because *you* matter.

Emma Byrne (11)
St Francis Of Assisi Catholic Technology College, Aldridge

Racism In Football

Racism is evil in football indeed
A horrible weed in God's garden that will go away
They're killing the soul of the black and white players
Not realising the pain inflicted on the people they attack
Football is meant to be a fun game without all the wicked football chants
Some fans are killing the game, those evil, crooked people
As they go home on the bus or train, they will claim that they weren't racist, but really they're liars
Sick and twisted and stupidly insane.

Henry Howell (11)
St Francis Of Assisi Catholic Technology College, Aldridge

You Are A Bully

You are a bully
You have everyone below you
You think that they are your friends
But really, they are just scared of you

You think you are in charge
But when someone bigger than you
Comes along
You scurry away, out of view

You think you can make me scared
Or make me insecure
But all you have done
Is make me more aware

If you think you have got me down
Or made me hide away
But all you have done
Is made me stronger

You are a bully.

Tamzin Timperley (12)
St Francis Of Assisi Catholic Technology College, Aldridge

The Smaller Ones

There's the second one
He's the one most like me
He can be my friend, my enemy
But I love him

Then there's the third one
The loud one
He can be angry, happy, sad
But I love him

Then there's the fourth one
The perfectionist
It's her way or no way
But I love her

And I'm the first one
The argument stopper and starter
I'm there whether they like it or not
After all, I'm the big brother

Family is family.

Cian James Hennessy (13)
St Francis Of Assisi Catholic Technology College, Aldridge

Bullying

Why are you such a bully?
You can see I'm hurting inside
I don't think you understand fully
I just wanna run away and hide

I just wonder why you pick on me
Did I do something wrong...?
I see you laugh and point at me
This is not where I belong

I know I can talk to my teachers
My parents, my family and friends
To tell them how you make me feel
Please let this bullying end

I'd rather be a little nobody
Than an evil somebody
So please stop!

Sarone Mengisteab (11)
St Francis Of Assisi Catholic Technology College, Aldridge

Why Do You Bully Me? It's Really Unkind

Why do you bully me? It's really unkind
I'm only human, why wouldn't I mind?
When you tease me, I feel sad
The feelings inside me are not good, they're bad
Sticks and stone may break my bones
But names will never hurt me
That's just not true, I'm sad, I'm hurt
I can't believe that you can't see
I may be different, I may be meek
But that doesn't mean I am weak
You think you're clever, you think you're strong
But soon, you'll realise you are wrong.

Madeleine Relihan (12)
St Francis Of Assisi Catholic Technology College, Aldridge

What Really Matters

A passing smile which brightens your day
A friendly 'hello' helps the blues away
A hug, a prayer, a cupcake or two
Makes the world seem kind and beautiful

Imagine a place filled with rainbows and unicorns
Your heart bursting with pride and hope
Your imagination lets you be anything you desire
Every day they can help you fly with a kind word as you pass by

A friendly pet reminds you with a simple purr
That life is wonderful if you surround yourself
With what really matters
Family and friends.

Harrison Stage Murray (12)
St Francis Of Assisi Catholic Technology College, Aldridge

Stop Bullying

Bullies are a huge problem
We really need to stop them
Making fun of you for being skinny or fat
Discriminating for things other than that

Making fun of you and ruining your day
All you can do is try not to get in their way
Words can kill if you're not careful
Just to make you think that you're powerful

If you're a bully
You're not cool
All you're doing is being cruel

If you ever see a bully
No matter how bad it seems
Always report them to someone
By any means.

Damian Biernacki (11)
St Francis Of Assisi Catholic Technology College, Aldridge

When I Was Younger

When I was younger, I dreamt of being a keeper
owning my own zoo with a lion called Brian
some lively tigers and even spiders
There'd be some funky monkeys and elephants
that were very intelligent
plus, a giraffe to make me laugh
but now I am older, I have changed my mind and
would rather watch them all free to roam and climb
and have a good time in the wild
where they've belonged since the beginning of time
I hope one day that people will learn to respect the world
and these wonderful animals who were all here first.

Louie James Timmins (11)
St Francis Of Assisi Catholic Technology College, Aldridge

One Life, One World

No one deserves the pain
The constant heartache
Heartless violence crumbles the world around us
If we let it crumble, there will be nothing left

Rise above the hatred
So that we receive no loss
Remember, we are united
Because God created us

Some happy families are no more
No mothers or fathers because of war
There's no reason for so much anger among us
Do you run, watch your agony is sore

One life, one world
Everything's to lose
Kindness doesn't cost
It's your life, you choose.

Vivienne Ince (13)
St Francis Of Assisi Catholic Technology College, Aldridge

In A World

I live in a world with white surroundings
I live in a world where I stand out from the crowd
I live in a world of fear and injustice
I live in a world where I can't speak out.

I live in a world with restrictions and boundaries
I live in a world where I am treated like dirt
I live in a world where I am judged immediately
I live in a world with unfairness and no hope.

I live in a world where I am always left out
I live in a world where I am never free
But I don't live in an imaginary world, I live in this world
And this is the world I fear most.

Aine-May Mulcrow (11)
St Francis Of Assisi Catholic Technology College, Aldridge

A First World War Poem

In the trenches, cold and wet
All around us, deaths were met
Every hour, brave heroes fell
The sights and sounds were just like Hell

Gas attacks that cause a stench
Grey, lined faces fill the trench
Thundering shells, so loud and piercing
Bombs that fall with smoke and hissing

Our uniforms are full of lice
And everywhere run rats and mice
Bodies lie just where they died
We want to run away and hide

The war has ended, the allies won
Silent graves, our lives are done
Poppies grow on dark, dry land
This was not the death we planned.

Kian Doody (11)
St Francis Of Assisi Catholic Technology College, Aldridge

Is Bullying Worth It?

People bully, anyone can be a victim
Why? Is bullying addictive?
Why must those people choose between silence or hate?
No one has the right to decide others' fate

They feel frightened and lonely
All their 'friends' are gone
So would they really choose to fight back
When they're all alone?
Home is the safest place
But for some people, that's not the case...

You may not use actions and just use words
But cruel words are like weapons - they really hurt
So be careful of the words you say
As they can leave scars that will never fade.

Alisha Karvnanycike (13)
St Francis Of Assisi Catholic Technology College, Aldridge

Air

Air is magical, like you and me
We can discuss it over a cup of tea
Leaves fly in the air
While flying around a Christmas fair
Dance outside, feeling the cold air against your face
Don't forget to tie up your shoelace
Air is needed by every living thing
Birds need it to fly with their wings
Air is made from lots of chemicals, some big, some small
Let's face it, we, as living things, need them all
Air is seen from ground to space
Things that fly may bring a smile to your face
If we don't look after the air we breathe
We're sure to suffer: this you can believe!

Emilia Tilly Wassell (12)
St Francis Of Assisi Catholic Technology College, Aldridge

My Poem

War, I do not get it
War, I do not like it
War, why is it here?
War, why is it happening?
War, why can't we be calm?
War, why can't it be stopped?
War, why don't you cry?
War, how don't you cry?
War, why are you not sad?
War, you need to stop
War, you destroy lives
War, you end many lives
War, you destroy towns
It makes no sense
It ends us all
How can humans make all of these?
Why do we all fight each other?
For nothing?
Why do we make these guns?
Why are they made to kill our friends?
Can't we all be friendly?
War, I do not like it.

Ethan Sivier (11)
St Francis Of Assisi Catholic Technology College, Aldridge

I Will Always Get The Blame

It starts with a nudge and a bit of a flick
Then a slap and a bit of a kick
That turns into a slap and a hit
Now I start to hurt a bit

Now he marches into my room
My face falls with gloom
But still, he can't take the hint
So it was quite a long stint

He wrestles me to the floor
I bang my head against the door
Mum shouts from the garden
"Still think you're bold and brazen?
Get out of his way
Or I'll ruin your day!"

She'll always side with him
Even when it's rather grim
This is why I have no shame
Because it's always me who gets the blame.

Sarah Morgan
St Francis Of Assisi Catholic Technology College, Aldridge

You Left

You left, walked out the door
not one single goodbye
Yet you still ruin everything
Rule over my life
I hear our song on the radio
that just seems to reply
and I want it to be meaningless
just to go away
but it seems to be stuck
just like gum in my hair
because no matter how hard I try
you'll always be there
till I can't stand you anymore
You just won't go away
but I guess it's not your fault
just fate's cruel way
of trying to remind me that I lost you
That I lost you that day
So one final time, I'll say goodbye
because I'm really sick of you
Wish our memories would die.

Millie Lavin
St Francis Of Assisi Catholic Technology College, Aldridge

The Reality Of Today

Discrimination
All we do is say we will put an end to it
But do we ever try?
All we do is ignore the reality of today...
All we do is ignore the fact that people are being ridiculed for their race, their faith, their sexual preferences or social status

Empty promises...
Broken communities...
Hopelessness...

It's unfair and we should speak out
Our society needs hope...
We need faith...

Being a young person in our world is difficult
We have so much to say... but they won't listen... she's just a child, they say

I'm a child who has much to say...
And I want to change our tomorrow, today.

Naomi Aliu (12)
St Francis Of Assisi Catholic Technology College, Aldridge

As the sun sets, and
the day comes to close
- I can't get the sand
out of my toes!

Isobel Grant (11)
St Francis Of Assisi Catholic Technology College, Aldridge

The Seaside

A desert of sand
Is the only land
A creature's eyes can see

Children are playing
Having fun
The usual sportsman
Having a run

Deckchairs are laid in rows
of ten - Grandad's fallen
asleep again!

Dad's blowing armbands
For his excited child
Mother's praying for them
not to get wild

The whisper of the sea
Splashing near, the crashing
of waves along the pier

Lifeguards ready with
whistles and floats
To save the fisherman
in their boats

Bullying

B ullies are just doing it to make themselves feel strong and powerful
U nderstand that they are not the stronger person, they are scared inside
L earn how to stand up to them and make sure that you speak out - don't stay silent
L isten to someone, if they reveal that they are being bullied, encourage them to talk to someone
Y ou are unique and special, no one has the right to treat you badly
I nsecure feelings make bullies think that they can make others feel isolated
N ever accept that bullying is the way to go, get help if you are the bully!
G row into a kind, generous, loving person - the person you were always meant to be.

Dara Anderson (11)
St Francis Of Assisi Catholic Technology College, Aldridge

My Christmas Wish

My Christmas wish for Santa
Well, this is how it goes
To bring to me with Rudolph
And his light, red, shiny nose

I only have one special wish
That's really precious to me
But I think they will be a bit too big
To put under my tree

I never got to see my nannies
Which really was a shame
Because God took them to Heaven
Sometime before I came

They really were so happy
I still love them so much
I will never forget them in my mind
And I will always stay in touch

That's my special wish for Santa
That would make me as happy as can be
To come down on Christmas morning
And see them standing by my tree.

Eilish O'Reilly
St Francis Of Assisi Catholic Technology College, Aldridge

Opening Up

It is not easy opening up
Even in written words, it's hard
I keep my door closed
And I lock it with a smile

I do not open up
Telling someone you care
Makes you vulnerable
And I can't have my heart broken again

I am awful at opening up
Because words are too powerful
I am selfish with my feelings
Because I can't trust anyone else with them

Sometimes I open up
I let go of what I've hidden away
Once I do this, my heart isn't protected
And anyone could do anything to hurt it

I am too cautious about opening up
Once your feelings are free
They could hurt anyone
And I can't let the people I love get hurt.

Millie Anne Kilgallen (13)
St Francis Of Assisi Catholic Technology College, Aldridge

Cancer

She killed a few of my family
She captured one of my friends
She goes around leaving scars
Collecting her jar of torn hearts
She comes and goes in what seems like a second
She makes our lives a misery

She takes innocent people
And terrorises them one by one
Slow and painful
That's how the dreaded deed is done
It sends a tear to my eye when I think about her
All the pain
All the grief
All the lives lost because of her
Why would something so horrible haunt us?

This needs to stop
No more pain
No more grief
No more lives lost because of her
We need to stick together
We need to fight back
And eventually
It *will* stop
We *will* fight back
We *will* stop cancer.

Isabelle Welch (12)
St Francis Of Assisi Catholic Technology College, Aldridge

Bullying

Bullying is bad and causes people pain
They think the more they do it, the more happiness they gain
Tears falling down their eyes, but you bullies don't care
You keep pushing and pushing till they can't bear
It might start as a joke but in the end, it isn't funny
Now they are miserable, their life is never sunny
No more rainbows now, it's just grey clouds
Now they have stopped eating because they feel they're not allowed
You see bullying causes problems, physical and mental
All this was started by something accidental
So all bullies out there, please stop because it causes harm
And it can even lead to cutting a leg or an arm
Yes, only a few words can lead to this, so don't
Bullies, we won't let you win, we just won't.

Caitlin Hall (12)
St Francis Of Assisi Catholic Technology College, Aldridge

A Land

A land of terror, a land of fear
A land very far away from here
Bombs boom and children cry
Are you still prepared to let them die?

What if it was you, alone and scared?
How would you feel if no one cared?
Skin withered and lips bright blue
If you were them, what would you do?

The Earth is a present to be shared
The inhabitants of it must be prepared
Out of the darkness, the innocent must be led
Or else they'll all end up dead

With their poor clothes tattered
Their last hope shattered
Feeble children washed upon the shore
Helpless, frail... alive no more

I think my message is very clear
We need to welcome the suffering here
Alone, we are useless... but together
We can save humanity forever and ever.

Molly Abigail Cope (12)
St Francis Of Assisi Catholic Technology College, Aldridge

but who'll let you know
you don't need to hide

someday, you'll go along
and see how far you've gotten
you thought you were alone
but in the end, *you'll see you are not.*

Esther Omokorede (13)
St Francis Of Assisi Catholic Technology College, Aldridge

Never Alone

Can you tell me
or let me see
all the things
you don't want to be

the hardest thoughts
the deepest wounds
the deepest cuts
your mind consumes

let me be there
just by your side
not leading the way
but still helping to guide

when there is no other way
we'll make a road
to tell your story
and lighten the load

and maybe this won't last
and I will have to go
but there will be someone else
who will also know

the pain and the sadness
you can't seem to set aside

I am so insecure
Why do I care about them?

I am beautiful
I am funny
I am friendly
I am brave
I am powerful
I am strong
I am me
And I like me

I am good enough.

Annie Hattersley (13)
St Francis Of Assisi Catholic Technology College, Aldridge

Why Am I Not Good Enough?

They are looking at me again...
Why am I not good enough?
Why do I get bullied?
Why am I so insecure?
Why am I so worried?
Why am I so afraid?
Why do I not want to go to school?
Why is it me?
Why am I not good enough?

They are still looking and talking...
Am I fat?
Am I too thin?
Am I spotty?
Is my voice too deep?
Or is it too high?
Am I fitting in with the latest trends?
Have I put on too much make-up?
Do I need to put on more?
Is my skirt too short?
Or is it too long?
Why are they still staring at me?

Why am I not good enough?
I did nothing to deserve this

All party leaders asked to come together to find a way forward

How are we all going to prosper from here thereafter?

Alex Richards (13)
St Francis Of Assisi Catholic Technology College, Aldridge

Brexit

Brexit! Brexit! Brexit!
British exit
The uncivil exit
MPs quarrelling exit
No-deal exit

May at her hardest
Corbyn at his awkwardest
Labour and Conservatives
Parliament preservative
The UK and Gibraltar left
in confusion
EU's permanent exclusion

On the news, night and day
Like the trains, there might be a slight delay
Children left frazzled
Concerned about their future, their careers, dreams and opportunities awaiting
The freedom of movement between the European countries
The shops and businesses, the small and mighty
Left anxiously waiting, wildly and withering
An hour goes swiftly like a dream, then we wait to see...

The Ayes to the right 202, the Noes to the left 432
What now are our hopes?
The Confidence Motion, 325 to 306

Does it seem real?
Do you want to help them?
Or do you want to forget them?
Will you save them?
Or will you ignore them?

Phoebe Hastings (12)
St Francis Of Assisi Catholic Technology College, Aldridge

Poverty Is A Problem!

Imagine you are in Africa's cruellest desert
Where your throat is dry as sand
Longing for some water
Oh, that would be grand

Your eyes are bloodshot-red
Your stomach, swollen and rumbling
You want to cry but you have no tears left
Your life has nearly finished crumbling

All you see around you is dying friends
Who could live no more without water
All you can hear is the sound of weeping mothers
Who have just lost their son or daughter

You pray to the Lord for some water
So you don't have to drink the wet mud
You pray that others see you are dying
And you pray that the Lord sends a flood

How long have you got left?
Will it be hours, days or weeks?
You only have a drop of hope left
Are you just too weak?

Stop imagining
How does it feel?
Do you feel guilty?

But the rose is a rose
And was always a rose
But the theory now goes
That the apple is the rose

There's the thing I shouldn't do
and yet, and now I have
the rest of the day to
make up for, not
undo, what can't be done
but next time
think more calmly
breathe, say, here's a new
morning, morning
morning.

Arronveer Patter (12)
St Francis Of Assisi Catholic Technology College, Aldridge

Feelings

Roses are red and violets are blue
But my heart seems to have a devil's flu
It beats as normal but doesn't smile as others do
Even in the ways, I try
I feel that my soul has died
When it laughs
It does in sorrowful times
When someone dies
When someone cries
When everyone says their goodbyes

If only there was such a way
That I could decontaminate my ways
A heart like an angel
A heart that God has
If only there was a method regarded as
And then the day came
When the risk
To remain tight
in a bud
was more painful
than the risk
it took
to blossom
I was infuriated when
My anger got stupendous again

When all my items are on the floor
She calls it mess, I call it art - I like art

Well, before I go, I need to tell you
About Gizmo, he's my dog
A very yappy one, if that's the word?
Anyway, he is the love of my life
For the rest of my life!

Alfie Stanley-Gough (12)
St Francis Of Assisi Catholic Technology College, Aldridge

Welcome To A Typical Day Of Alfie Stanley-Gough!

Well, there is no typical day for me!
Maybe I should have named this
The life of Alfie Stanley-Gough
Because every day is different
Some are good, some are bad

Well, where should I start?
Is there a main part?
Well, my day usually starts by
My mum, dropping a morning fart!

So, let's say it's Saturday morning
And because I'm a really nice person
I sometimes let my mum have a lie-in
Well, she thinks I'm being nice
But all I want to do is play on my Xbox
Ssshh, don't tell her

I love it when Mum says, "Shall we go for something to eat as a breakfast treat?"
Well, how was I supposed to know
Butter and a toaster do not mix?
You'll end up having something to fix

I have a massive thing for clothes
Although my mum doesn't understand

Ever so close
Would peace ever come?

Boom! The world went quiet
Peace, peace had come
Still, we would never be whole
For so many did not return
"Lest we forget."

Boom! Today, the world is loud again
As if it never stopped
Still, violence and hatred
Still injustice and prejudice
Will it ever stop?

Isabella Faye Rounds (13)
St Francis Of Assisi Catholic Technology College, Aldridge

Wars

Boom! Echoes of bombs shake my nerves
Still, I see the images of people I used to know
Marching off in lines, like ants
Mother stroking my hair as they left
"Not much longer."

Boom! It never stops
It unfolded as if a box before me
Would they come home?
Would they return?
I did not know

Boom! went the front line
Brave men at each own position
Hoping and praying
That there was a God above
"Protect me, please."

Boom! The drum-like sounds never stopped
Bullets raced towards us
Would this ever stop?
When would it all be over?
"When the battles are fought and won."

Boom! Down in the trenches
Ever closer we were
To the battle being won

I've finished my poem and I have done my bit
Let me ask you a question, is it worth it?

Matthew Dowd (12)
St Francis Of Assisi Catholic Technology College, Aldridge

Is It Worth It?

To all the bullies out there
I have a message for you
You pick on certain people and think it's fine
Understand that doing this is not right
How could you treat another person like that and make them upset?
Your cold heart gets satisfaction out of this with no regret - is it worth it?
Imagine having to wake up every day, trembling with fear of what today will bring
Meeting that person, knowing that they will treat you like dirt, not a human thing
Thinking that you're big and to a person, being really mean
Big person, are you? Can't say it to their face so you say it behind a screen - is it worth it?
Physical, verbal, social and cyber, there are all types of bullying
You do this and it is not of the human nature
And being a bully, you're also a hater
Make fun of the person for the way they may look and the way they may dress
You say their life is bad but to be so mean, your life is a mess. Is it worth it?
I'm done with you now, I have said what I can to try to teach you
Listen to me, don't be like that, change your life, start anew

Butterflies soaring around my room,
A picture of a man and woman riding their bikes by a turquoise stream,
Wishing the world was like a bright and colourful dream

Around my room, I dance and dance,
Hoping for raindrops at first glance,
Also for the sun, so mighty and bright,
Wishing for a rainbow to appear that night,
I never thought about writing poetry,
But it was easy for this poem was about me,
How my life can have highs, like a soaring sea.

Amy Rose Weir (12)
St Francis Of Assisi Catholic Technology College, Aldridge

Like A Soaring Sea

On Monday, I sign up
Tuesday, I buy the kit
Wednesday, I have a try
Thursday, make the team
Friday, I make new friends
Saturday, I have my first match
Sunday is my favourite day to play netball

The week after,
I buy a cat,
I call her Zee-Zee,
She cuddles up close whenever she's frightened,
I stroke her until she's satisfied,
She comforts me when I'm sad,
And her personality is a small reflection of mine

This month, I go to the shopping centre,
I buy a sketchpad and some art supplies,
When I arrive home, I start drawing,
I am finished when an hour has gone by,
Looking at my masterpiece,
Proud of what I have done,
Thanking God that he gave me this talent

My room was also done that day,
The colours of yellow and grey,
Yellow like the savannah and grey like the moon,

Let's stop wasting electricity
And start to take action to reduce global warming
Our world is in danger, but only if someone would listen

There's no future upon us
Unless we make a change
These impacts will continue to grow
And create costly damage to our world
A world we cannot replace
Affecting all of us in society
A community, including me and you
Let's make a change to this world before it's too late
Our world is in danger, but hopefully, someone will listen.

Sophie Doocey (13)
St Francis Of Assisi Catholic Technology College, Aldridge

Global Warming

I shed a tear for our land
The use of fuels is making it harder for us to live
A world full of pollution, no longer a drop of clean air
A land, no longer green, yet only black skies I seem to see
Our planet is getting warmer and warmer
Yet people seem to think that it is rather nice
Our world is in danger, but only if someone would listen

Evil is taking over the forests
Making it harder for animals to live
Constant sight of fear that spreads through the atmosphere
The fear of having no home, no sense of comfort or security
Our world is in danger, but only if someone would listen

Rising sea levels, coastal floods, droughts are upon us
Unavoidable weather, sudden wildfires
And heatwaves are no longer rare to us
Who knows what else is to come
Damaging chemicals fill the ocean and consume the clean air
All because of climate change that we are causing
Our world is in danger, but only if someone would listen

But maybe we could stop deforestation
And wasting water too
Let's try to recycle more
Not throw away old objects that could still have good use

They ignored what I said and both ran away
I felt like they were the predators and I was the prey

When I got home, I didn't tell my mum
If I did, I would feel quite dumb
When I was locking the door with my key
I thought to myself, *are they bullying me?*
Tomorrow is Friday and I don't want to go to school
If they see me, I will feel like a fool
Here comes another long school day ahead
"You can make it through today," I said.

Erin McIntyre (13)
St Francis Of Assisi Catholic Technology College, Aldridge

My Story

I never knew words could hurt me, until yesterday
I was walking down the road, and then I heard a 'hey'
I didn't know who it was at first, so then I turned around
After I saw who it was, I had quite a frown
It was my best friend, with someone I do hate
I tried to walk away, but it was already too late
My best friend had betrayed me and stabbed me in the back
So, I tried to carry on walking, but they shouted me to come back
I decided to turn around, to see what they had to say
They started calling me names and were treating me the wrong way
I started to cry and carry on with my way home
But on the way there, I felt like I wasn't alone
I didn't turn around and carried on walking
But in the distance, I could hear someone talking
As I could hear it more and more
I just carried on and tried to ignore
Finally, I turned around, to see what it could have been
It was the same two girls and they were still being mean
They started to laugh, and one ran in front of me
they both tripped me up and I fell onto my knee
As they both laughed, I turned and said
"What have I ever done to you?" as I shook my head

Everyone's missing you
No one wanted you to go
We all need you right now
Your name is everywhere
All around the town
People bringing you bouquets of flowers to our door
Your brother, your sisters, your mom, your fiance, your nieces and nephews, your children
Everyone is proud of you
Not a day goes by without someone thinking about you

I love you, my precious auntie
I hope you're proud of me
I hope you're smiling down
And I will never forget to draw you on the family tree
It's been two months now since you left this world too good for you
And I hope to see you one day when I come up too.

Benita Jaeneke (12)
St Francis Of Assisi Catholic Technology College, Aldridge

My Beautiful Auntie

Sometimes, life isn't always fair
It takes things that we love away from us
As we look at the pictures and blow off the dust
We remember the memories we had together
The day that you got your dog
The day that I was blessed when you came into my life
I didn't anticipate losing you so young
I wanted you to live forever
A cruel disease took you away from me and all of the family
Why did you have to go?
Why right now, when I need you the most?
I will remember that you will always be in my heart

One day, when I have children of my own
I will tell them what an inspiration you were towards us
Thank you for always being there through thick and thin
And whenever I see a rainbow, I sneak a little grin

You fought with that disease for so long
Not a day went past when you didn't give up your fight
All I want in life right now is for you to come back to me
I want to give you one last hug and say goodbye properly
I want to tell you how much I love you
How much you mean to me

Female Equality

It's all about the numbers
750 million women and girls were married before they were eighteen
200 million woman and girls in thirty countries have endured female mutilation
It's all about the numbers

It's all about the numbers
Forty-nine countries lack laws protecting women from domestic violence
One in five women and girls have experienced physical or sexual violence
It's all about the numbers

It's all about the numbers
Only twenty-three percent are women in parliament
Globally, women are only thirteen percent landholders
It's all about the numbers

It's all about the numbers
We are one hundred percent certain things should change
We are one hundred percent certain you wouldn't want these things happening to yourself or your daughters
We are one hundred percent certain that we need to do better globally
It's all about the numbers.

Violet-May Green (12)
St Francis Of Assisi Catholic Technology College, Aldridge

You're free to do whatever you want
You like to be alone...

Luca Sadler (12)
St Francis Of Assisi Catholic Technology College, Aldridge

The thoughts of what they might do to you
It's making you start frettin'

Along the way back home
It's jolly but it's sad
You're happy that you've escaped
But your mood is turning bad
Bruises mentally and physically
Are hurting you like mad
You feel miniature and weak
'Cause you're only a young lad

You make it to the front door
Weakened at your core
You put your mask on
Like your life is happiness galore

The real truth, it hurts inside
You don't want your parents to worry
You put your fears, your thoughts aside
You pull open the door in a hurry

You bolt upstairs to your room
To flee from all reality
You lie down on your bed
To forget the pain, the agony

You feel a sense of happiness
Because you're on your own

Alone

Along the way to school
You're dreading to start the day
You really hate the thought of being
Hunted as the prey

The walk feels even longer
With each and every thought
Of being bullied every day
You just can't take it anymore

The bumps and bruises
The repulsive words
They're starting to wear you down
You're being bullied several times
It's giving you a frown

The tears, the sweat
Are drip-dropping from your face
You used to enjoy being at school
Now you're starting to hate this place

Walking down the hall
On the way to your next lesson
You see them marching towards you
You're anxious and you're stressin'
You don't know what they want
You don't know what they're gettin'

My Moment

Waiting, waiting, waiting...
Adrenaline coursing through my veins
Every nerve end tingling inside me
My heart thuds, interrupting the deafening silence
As I contemplate this moment, the culmination of my whole life's hard work

The hard work, the blood, the sweat and the tears shed in training
Yes, they have all led to this moment
The biggest moment of my life
This is my chance, my moment, a showcase of what I can do

The enormity of this moment hits me like an iron fist
Pressure weighs down heavy on me
I've lived out this moment over and over in my head but nothing compares now to the reality I face
I say to myself, "This is my time, and I can do this."

It's time, I take my first steps out onto the field
It's like a weight lifting off my shoulders
I settle myself, relax, allowing myself to drink in the intoxicating atmosphere
I repeat... my time, my chance to show the world what I can do.

James Culshaw (12)
St Francis Of Assisi Catholic Technology College, Aldridge

Germans cheering, some wondered what the retreating was all about
Then came our air support, the bomb that wiped them all out

Many years have passed, we won and the war was finally over
The memorial had commenced, outside of Dover
It made me think back to Jackson's fate
And his final words, "No mission too difficult, no sacrifice too great."

Marco Sadler (13)
St Francis Of Assisi Catholic Technology College, Aldridge

They stood speechless, spotting the scary ton of the flanks
Of our Pershing, Stuart and Sherman tanks

We had them outsmarted, outwitted, until the tank drivers
Were beaten by the German Panzers, Panthers and Tigers
As quick as lightning, Jackson being no buffoon
Got on the radio yelling, "Come in, this is the 1st platoon!"

"Affirmative, Hawkeye 3-2 en route, we're coming.
This'll be painful, you'd better start running."
Orders were carried out, we started to retreat
We set a rendezvous point where hopefully we'd meet

On the run, we found ourselves, not to get shot I begged.
Commander Jackson was shot in the leg
He told me to go before it was too late
"No mission too difficult, no sacrifice too great."

I dashed agile and quick
The toxic wind thrown at my face, made me feel sick
I saw Jackson fighting his last stand
A bullet penetrated his skin, his pistol rolled from his hand

He lay, lifeless, deceased and, inanimate, there I stood
Gaping at his body, in a bath of his own blood
I recoiled in horror, at the sight of this, I ran away
An open field, no cover, somewhere I didn't want to stay

As I was climbing up a hill, away from the fight
I caught a glimpse, one last sight

No Mission Too Difficult, No Sacrifice Too Great

Marching into warfare, many of us would find
This was a one-way journey, our families left behind
The journey was distant, the ground was sloppy
The ambience was intimidating, the winds were choppy

There my comrades marched, determined and tenacious
And Commander Jackson, who stood beside us
He was dedicated to life on the front line, and substantial training
Experienced combatant, hardly ever complaining

Then, we stumbled across a war-torn battlefield, everyone fell silent and sombre
A horrible spectacle, then we observed what lay yonder
Many soldiers fighting, many brave souls had died
A Private shouted at the sight of us, "Our reinforcements have arrived!"

All of us scrambled, sped, sprinted, to their aid, my gun desperately escaping my hand
As I ran with my firearm, my shield, my M1 Garand
Our army fought strong, as strong as steel
Fighting like this to me was surreal

We had the advantage, with our method of oppression
Our fierce, ferocious attitude, frightened our opponent with aggression

Generation Zombie

My mom thinks we're becoming a generation of zombies
As soon as we're plugged in and switched on, we're isolated from this realm
Zoned out and obsessed with completing the game
Hands gripped tight on the controller, excited, heart pumping, head spinning, you're at the helm

But gaming can be good, it's not all negative
It helps with coordination, problem-solving, you could even go as far as saying it is good for your education

It can even teach you how to play different sports and activities
It may even help you find your future occupation

The dark side of gaming is violent shoot-em-ups
People get lost in a warped reality
Hiding behind a facade to keep up with your peers
Gamers become immune to the brutality

Xbox, PS4, Nintendo all need to protect and take more responsibility
They are making bucket loads of money
The person with the controller needs parental control and guidance to stay safe online
Generation zombie would not be so funny.

Blaise Mich'eal River Delahunty-Forrest (12)
St Francis Of Assisi Catholic Technology College, Aldridge

This is based on a real event
I hope my bully will read and repent.

Caitlin Jefferis (11)
Our Lady & St Chad Catholic Academy, Wolverhampton

Without You

You made me feel like a no one
That I was the ugly one
You made me feel that I was bad
Just because you were mad
You destroyed me completely
At least now I'm free
You made me lose all confidence
I'm glad I'm away from you, so good riddance
I thought you were my friend
But then it started to end
You told me I was fat
You made me believe that
You ruined my life
And left it in strife

Now I'm away from you, I am amazing
And there is no way you are fazing
Me any more
To me, you are just a piece of mud on the floor
Now I am a total queen
You are just stupid and mean
I am quirky and unique
I feel so sorry for you, so stupid and weak
I am superior
You are inferior

Don't end your life...
I'm with you all the way.

Chloe Sereneo (11)
Our Lady & St Chad Catholic Academy, Wolverhampton

My Best Friend

You see that girl under the bridge?
She cries all the time
but her words always lie
When everyone is asking, "Why?"
She just wants to die

Her screams are shouts for help
Everyone shrugs and says, "Welp?"
Her pills are overflowing
Without anyone knowing

The bridge is her outlet
She's meeting her demise
She's got a happiness debt
I don't know
if she's going to make
it out alive

Here I am now, my
best friend is dead
I'm in complete dread
I don't have a reason
to live
I have nothing else to give

Depression isn't a phase
It's not just one bad day
Life for them is strife